Full Circle

How to Become a Victor in Life

Devin H. Pipkin

Full Circle

Independently published
Copyright © 2019, Devin H. Pipkin

Published in the United States of America

171127-00965--3

ISBN-13: 978-1796663037

For more information on 90-Minute Books including finding out how you
can publish your own book, visit 90minutebooks.com or call (863) 318-0464

Here's What's Insid

Dedicated to my parents,

Dr. Larry H. Pipkin

Martha Sharon Pipkin

The best examples of loving, caring parents I have ever seen. Without them, I would not have made it through life as I have and most assuredly would not have been able to view my life's journey as I do.

Introduction

You might wonder what I mean, exactly, by "full circle."

My passion for life has grown and thrived despite much adversity. This has happened largely due to multiple realizations I've had over the years— which you'll learn more about within these pages. I doubt I was ever alone in this feeling, but at one point, I often felt like my life was a book—one that I was a character in, rather than the author of.

But gradually, as I observed those around me a little more carefully, I grew to understand that both good *and* bad things happened to them, too. Some of these people were more vocal than others, but most, like me, struggled with how to deal with the bad things life throws at us. Many played the victim well, even in small ways, such as plodding through the days instead of savoring each moment: "Ugh, it's Monday! Oh, Mondays are awful."

When it comes to our inner voices—the language we use when we talk to ourselves—I find that many give in to temptation and take a defeatist tone, rather than looking within for inspiration and drive. When others talk about themselves or their future with such negative words, all I can think of is, "Wow, you have so much power!" Adversity has taught me that you can turn around your entire mindset and lift yourself from negativity by using different words in this inner monologue—and also by carefully considering how you talk about yourself out loud.

I've always been one of those people who always want to help. That's part of why I was drawn to the field of insurance, a mechanism most people don't like and don't understand (plenty of people feel that they're trapped into spending a lot of money on it that's wasted if the worst-case scenario doesn't happen, and that it's the lesser of two evils—the greater evil being financial catastrophe, of course).

Since childhood, I've also been fascinated by the wonder of construction. I'd long planned to have a career as a contractor, but as you'll see, that was not to be. But when I discovered that I could combine these fundamental elements of myself—that drive to help and to serve, and my unceasing interest in construction—it became clear to me that contractors would be the ones I would serve. As I gradually gained a better understanding of the field, it became apparent that my work would not only make a difference for the individual contractors, but the construction industry as a whole.

So along the way, I discovered a personal "secret sauce": a way to get through much of the bad stuff life will inevitably throw your way. And I was stunned by how simple it was. All of a sudden, I thought, "Wow, there it is! It's taken me decades to figure this out, but it really is easy. How can I help others discover this? How can I give them a huge head start on me?"

And that's what I mean by full circle. I hope that these pages will help you turn around negativity in your life and will inspire you to clearly see the incredible things adversity can lead you to achieve. Read on, and enjoy the book. To your success!

—Devin

My Story

The bicycle, borrowed from my older sister without permission, as found at the scene of the accident.

My purpose here is to help you understand that bad things happen to all of us. Often, what happens to us is beyond our control, but what we can control is the manner in which we respond to it and handle it. I hope my story inspires you to choose to be a victor, rather than a victim.

I was raised in an upper-middle-class, white-collar family. My father was a very successful practicing optometrist, and my mother stayed home to raise the kids. We were an extremely close family, and my parents were very loving.

Our parents taught us that we were fortunate, and we should always do for others before we did for ourselves. They ingrained in all of us a very strong work ethic: we learned that if we fell—or got knocked—down, we were expected to pick ourselves up and march on. These lessons they taught us as we grew up are at the heart of my story; I didn't realize just how often I'd apply them in my own life until much later.

My story spans a life time, but the heart of it began when I was thirteen years old. On October 1, 1976, I asked my parents if I could join my friend Todd on a bike ride to a K-Mart a couple of miles away. Appropriately, they told me no, but I was a thirteen-year-old boy, so I grabbed my sister's bike and went anyway.

On the way back from the store, about a half mile from home and maybe two hundred yards from the turn toward my house, a drunk driver traveling at seventy miles an hour ran off the road and hit me. The impact was so direct and so tremendous that the fibers of my jeans were imprinted on his steel bumper. When he hit me, I flew over the front of his car, off toward the passenger side. My head connected with the car's bullet-shaped side mirror and nearly flattened it.

According to an eyewitness, as the driver swerved back onto the road, the momentum catapulted my body thirty feet in the air—about sixty feet in terms of distance. On my way down, I struck the top of a road sign, hit the ground, and then tumbled on for another fifty to sixty feet. The driver swerved back onto the road and kept going, leaving me behind.

A crowd gathered, as several people who had seen the accident stopped to help. One gentleman used his CB radio to call the police. Witnesses reported that I quickly got up and began hopping around on my right leg—and that my left leg dangled beside it. I don't remember it, but several witnesses had to tackle me to hold me down.

At the same time, I remember other elements of the scene very clearly. There were many people around, and one woman sat behind me. As I lay there on my back, she leaned over me, rubbed my face and head, and tried to comfort me. She told me, "Everything's going to be fine. Relax. It's going to be okay." She held one of my hands tightly, and I remember that she made me feel safe.

Before the ambulance arrived, my father, along with one of my sisters and my younger brother, came upon the scene of the accident by chance. The road was closed, so the traffic had stopped; my family got out of my father's car to see what was happening. Imagine their surprise and terror at finding me lying in a tremendous pool of blood. I'd lost half the blood in my body, and one of my legs was splayed out at a right angle in the middle of my shin. It was reasonable for them to think I was dead.

Moments later, my other sister—the one whose bike I'd taken—left home for work. She arrived at the scene, spotted her bicycle lying by the side of the road, and drove her car straight into the ditch to find out what had happened.

The only member of my family who wasn't there was my mother; someone hurried to our house to get her, and she arrived before the ambulance as well. We were complete: my entire family was there to bear witness to this horror. As often as I've tried, I cannot imagine what went through their minds that afternoon, but I vividly remember seeing the mental pain and anguish my parents experienced as they watched over my recovery.

When the police and the ambulance finally arrived, somehow the scene became even more chaotic. They announced that they were going to take over, and that the people who had bravely provided me comfort needed to move back. I remember being a little uneasy with that, but it happened nonetheless.

The ambulance driver and two paramedics began to talk to me, telling me they were going to have to get me onto a stretcher. Exactly how they were going to do that was the challenge, as my leg was barely attached to my body—and they certainly didn't want to accidentally detach it at the scene.

They told me, "Devin, this is going to hurt a lot, but we need to get a splint on your leg, because it's been injured." A police officer knelt behind me, taking the place of the woman who'd been comforting me. He held down my hands behind my head as one of the paramedics grabbed my right leg and held down my shin and foot.

With that, the pain came. As they tried to straighten my leg, I let out a yell, drew my foot back out of his hands, and kicked him hard. The blow caught him right in the chest; he hit the ground and rolled backward, or so I'm told.

Eventually, they got me under control and into the ambulance. My mother climbed in with me, and off we went. The scene was only 10 minutes from the hospital, but I remember every single bump, regardless of how small they might have been. Each time we'd hit a bump, I'd let out a scream as phenomenal pain scorched through my entire body.

I remember yelling out to the driver: "You have to slow down! Don't hit the bumps! Or at least tell me when you're going to."

On Eighth Avenue, a set of three railroad tracks lies just before to the entrance to the emergency room. I remember the driver telling me, "Devin, we're coming up on some railroad tracks. I'm going to slow way down, but they're still kind of rough, so it's probably going to hurt." As he hit them, I blacked out.

Three days later, I regained consciousness in the ICU. When I woke up, my mother was next to me, holding my hand. Monitors surrounded me. I remember a tremendous amount of pain, but I couldn't tell where it was coming from. I knew some of it was in my leg, but it was all over my body, too. Everything hurt. Everything hurt.

My back was broken. My neck was broken. My head was severely lacerated. My left leg had compound fractures in six to ten places (which is why the splint's application had been so excruciating; in a multiple compound fracture, the bones are splintered).

I'm sure there were another couple of days in which I came in and out of consciousness and didn't know what was happening. After about a week, my mother was able to tell me that I'd been in a very serious accident and that I had some injuries.

But it wasn't until quite a bit later that I learned what the doctors had told my parents about my condition on the night of the accident, after they'd worried and waited during the three hours I spent in surgery. They were told not to leave my side, as the doctors were relatively certain I wouldn't make it through the weekend. They were told I would not survive.

The surgery had taken care of the trauma they could find—the broken bones and so on—but they believed that my internal injuries were probably very extensive, and they were unsure about where else I'd been injured. At the time, there was no way they could subject me to the exploratory surgery that would be necessary to find out.

For a while there, it was a wait-and-see situation. It seemed like a long road in the ICU, as doctors and nurses constantly came and went. I remember feeling very confused, and I'm sure I don't remember a lot of it.

Once I was finally released from the ICU, I took up residence on one of the "regular floors" for several weeks. Throughout my stay, I was very groggy, as I was on a lot of different kinds of medications. I'm unsure as to what drugs I received, but on many occasions, I had violent medication reactions that gave me terrible nightmares. Apparently, I'd grow violent in the night and knock over monitors. They were afraid

I'd hurt myself, so I'd occasionally wake up to find myself tied to the bed.

I had no idea what I'd done. Imagine waking up and finding yourself in the hospital, tied to your bed, and having no idea why. I was only thirteen. It was a confusing and very difficult time for me mentally.

The pain was constant. It never stopped. It was excruciating. It was incredibly hard to deal with—both physically and mentally—but I had to get through it. I had no choice. With or without the drugs, the pain was always there.

At times during my long recovery process, I often thought about what I could have done differently, what could have prevented me from being in the path of that car. Many things, I suppose—for one, I could have listened to my parents and not gone out at all, as they'd told me not to. Or I could have been riding in front, and then Todd would have been hit instead of me.

Or we could have left the store earlier. That's the one I always came back to.

Back in the day at K-Mart, the store would have events where mothers could bring in their babies to have portraits taken. The photographer had a setup right in the middle of the store, with a table to set the babies on and tons of props to get them to look at the camera and smile.

So on our way out, I spotted the photographer's little customers. I told Todd I wanted to stop and watch for a minute because the babies were so cute—the rolls of fat on their little legs and arms, and their jolly little laughs that made their chubby bellies wobble. They were just being themselves, with no idea of what was going on or why the funny man wanted them to look in a particular direction. I'm not sure which was more entertaining—the babies or the photographer who was maniacally waving the toys around and hopping up and down, just to get them to smile. We ended up staying to watch for about fifteen minutes and then took off for home.

As luck would have it, I was only five or so minutes from my turnoff when the driver hit me. If we hadn't stopped to look at the babies, the accident that changed my life never would have happened. For years afterward, my mind would flash from one picture to another, again and again—I would see myself watching the babies laugh and smile, and then the picture would shift to me lying in the ICU when I woke up a few days later.

My Mother's Gift: Magic

One of my early magic show props - an antique set of
Hippity Hop Rabbits.

I describe the time as I slowly healed in the hospital as "just surviving." I didn't give any thought to the future, nor did I know what the future held for me. I don't recall ever thinking, "When am I going to get out? When am I going to get better?" After a while, my spirits lifted a bit, and I accepted where I was.

But as you can imagine, I got very bored, so I began entertaining myself by tormenting nurses. In truth, it was pretty fun. I must stress that they were fun people, and that they were very kind to me. I'm sure they felt very sorry for me. Of course, I got to know a lot of them quite well because I was there for so long.

One nurse in particular, Diane, was willing to give me the room to tease her and play with her. I'd push my call button to get her to come to my room, and when she'd get there, I'd say, "Oh, I'm so confused. I forgot why I asked you to come in here. I'm sorry." Once she was ten steps or so out of the room, I'd hit the call button again. She'd return, and I'd say, "Oh, yeah, I remember. I wanted to say hi and see how you're doing today." Diane would roll her eyes. "Devin," she'd say.

After a while, that kind of stuff got boring, so I moved on to more fun activities. Sometimes I'd reach down and unplug one of the monitors, which would cause an alarm to go off at the nurses' station. They'd come running, and I'd claim that I had no idea what had happened.

Other times, I'd pull off the sticky leads that were attached to me, also causing alarms to go off.

But my favorite pastime was messing with the student nurses who came by to give me shots. The students were always quite nervous; in some cases, I was only the first or second person they'd ever given a shot to. I'd gotten this down to a routine: each time one would get ready to insert the needle, I'd let out a scream to scare the poor woman.

Eventually, my little act wore out its welcome. As one unlucky target administered a shot, my scream made her jump and accidentally toss away the needle. As she tried to recover, she stepped backward and tripped on the leg of chair—sending her down to the floor. With an audible smack, she landed right on her backside.

The young nurse wasn't hurt, but they told my mother, and I caught hell for that. My mother told me, "Cast or not, I can flip you over and spank your bottom if you do that kind of thing again."

As the weeks wore on, I continued to be bedridden. A mild depression would set in some days. From my hospital-room window, I could see kids come and go from the junior high school across the street. I wanted to be with them, back in the world, and out of that hospital, and that bed.

Although I'd never expressed any interest in before, my mother brought me a couple of magic books to help pass the time. One of the books was about rope tricks, so she brought along several feet of rope as well.

"Here, why don't you read these?" she said. "You'd probably be good at magic."

To this day, I don't know why she thought I'd be good at magic. I had never done anything like it before—in fact, I didn't seem to have any particular skills or hobbies. Ever since kindergarten, I'd been a C-minus student (as it turned out, my C-minus streak continued through high school). But my mom was trying to brighten my mood, so I said, "Okay, yeah, whatever, Mom."

The books sat by my bed for a couple of days. Once I finally picked one up and started reading it, I quickly got interested. One of the books covered the history of Erik Weisz, who later took the stage name of Harry Houdini. I learned how he trained himself to manipulate his body in amazing ways to permit his daring escapes and sword-swallowing stunts. He even figured out how to hide keys in his throat!

Since I had nothing but time on my hands, I started practicing some of the magic tricks. After a while, I mustered up the courage to show some of the magic tricks I'd learned to Diane, my favorite nurse.

She smiled and said, "Wow, that's good, Devin!"

I mumbled, "Yeah, whatever."

Diane was insistent. "No, honestly." She paused and then said, "Here, wait a minute."

She disappeared for a moment and returned with one of the other nurses. "Show her. She'll love it."

Encouragement was just what I needed. I performed the trick again, this time for a rapt audience of two.

The women lit up enthusiastically. "Wow!" "That's neat!"

I dedicated the next few days to more and more practice: sleight of hand stuff, some involving keys and coins; making things disappear; tricks involving foam balls; and other magic fundamentals. One day, some of the nurses brought in a younger kid in a wheelchair and asked me to show him some of my stuff—so I did, to his delight.

A while later, once I was finally able to get out of my bed and into a wheelchair, they'd wheel me in to the rooms of other patients who weren't mobile and couldn't get out. I found that I enjoyed entertaining others tremendously; the more often I did it, the more elaborate stories I would make up to tell alongside the tricks.

I realized that at best, I was probably a mediocre magician, but I so enjoyed making up and telling stories and all the patter that went along with the tricks that it didn't matter. It dawned on me that I'd discovered something that I was in fact quite good at.

I stuck with my new craft, practicing almost every day. By the time I got out of the hospital, I'd spent a year, to the week, in a cast, and I'd been either in bed, in a wheelchair, or on crutches the whole time.

One afternoon sometime after I got out of the hospital, my mother had a friend over. She saw me doing some of my magic tricks, and she was impressed.

"Hey, Devin, would you do some of your magic tricks for my son's fifth birthday party?"

I pondered the idea for a moment before responding. "Well, yeah. Sure. That'd be kind of fun."

I showed up at the party prepared, with a card table draped in a bed sheet (for the mystery factor). I put on a fifteen-minute show for the kids, who were amazed. They *loved* it. I got paid $15 or $20, and well, that was pretty cool, too.

At the party, three other moms approached me.

"Devin, you're so good! The kids love you. Would you do a show for my child's birthday party?"

I thought, "Sure, why not?"

Just like that, I was in business.

The Magic Pays Off

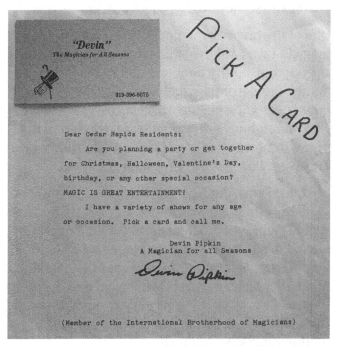

"*Devin*"
The Magician for All Seasons

319-396-8075

PICK A CARD

Dear Cedar Rapids Residents:

Are you planning a party or get together for Christmas, Halloween, Valentine's Day, birthday, or any other special occasion? MAGIC IS GREAT ENTERTAINMENT!

I have a variety of shows for any age or occasion. Pick a card and call me.

Devin Pipkin
A Magician for all Seasons

(Member of the International Brotherhood of Magicians)

My first advertisement for professional magic shows.

In the weeks that followed, I performed at the other three parties, and at each of *those* parties, more mothers asked me to perform for their kids' parties.

My little enterprise wasn't limited to kids' birthday parties. I was also asked to do a show at a church and for other groups. Pretty soon, I was having large-stage illusions shipped to me from England and France. By the time I was sixteen, I was doing half-hour shows in nightclubs for $75 a pop. Back in 1978, $75 for a half hour of work was really something.

One of my favorite memories from my time as a magician was a show at a fancy country club for a group of wealthy people. I don't recall the name of the group—and to this day I wonder how I ever got a gig like this, since I was a fifteen-year-old nobody—but they were dressed to the nines, in tuxes and formal gowns, and they were at least my parents' age or older.

So there I was, on the stage, with the show about to begin, and I had a problem: a grand piano was sitting right where I needed to set up a trick. I looked around for a club employee who could help me move it out of the way, but they'd all made themselves scarce. I shrugged and decided to move it myself. It seems easy enough, I thought—just get on one side of it and pull, or get on the other side and push.

Well, I tried pulling first. Nope. I tried pushing. That accomplished two things: One, I got the piano out of the way. Two: I broke one of the piano's legs. Just as I moved the piano clear of the space I needed, I heard the leg pop.

I plunged into a full-on panic. I skittered away from the piano, praying it wouldn't fall. It didn't, and the show went on.

Any time you're doing a live performance, you feel a lot of pressure, and you have to be prepared for anything. In this case, you can add to that the fact that I was performing in front of a bunch of rich people in fancy attire with, one would think, pretty high expectations, *and* I'd just broken a grand piano. My heart was pounding as the show began.

My first trick involved Lippincott boxes. If you've ever been to a magic show, chances are, you've seen this kind of trick. The trick, if done well and with good showmanship, is always a fun and exciting crowd-pleaser. There are two boxes involved in the trick: one larger box stays on the stage, neatly perched on a table, and a second smaller one is carried out into the audience, where the magician seeks out an "assistant" who seems willing to play along.

Both boxes have elaborate locks and (here's the secret) a side that slides away if you know exactly how to push on it. After the assistant closely examines the box and affirms its security to the crowd, the magician coaxes him or her to sacrifice an object of value, and it goes in the little box. The assistant locks the little box and keeps the key, and the magician carries the box back up to the stage. A bit of sleight of hand takes places as the magician slips the object out of the little box, slips it into the bigger one, and *voila*! The object magically disappears from the small box and reappears in the larger one. My Lippincott boxes were among the most expensive equipment I owned; they were handmade in Germany, and of the finest craftsmanship. I trusted them implicitly.

I scanned the well-heeled audience and thought of the perfect object to ask for: an engagement ring. It wasn't long before I found my ideal assistant: a woman with a huge smile who really seemed to be enjoying her evening.

I strolled up to her, showed her the box, and told her to lock and unlock it a few times, just to prove it was secure. I asked for her ring; she promptly placed it in the box and locked it up with a flourish.

I turned away from her and walked back to the stage, trying to slide away the false side of the box so the ring would drop into my hand. To my horror, it wouldn't give. I froze for a moment and searched my mind—*why isn't this working?*

Then it hit me: *The ring is too big.* The huge diamond took up too much space in the little box, and the false side was jammed. *Oh my God*, I thought. *What am I going to do?*

Well, like I said, any time you have a live performance, you have to be prepared for just about anything. Whatever happens, you have to roll with it. I reached the stage, still in a panic, and turned and looked out over the audience. I stared at them for a moment or two, and gradually let a puzzled look settle over my face.

Gradually, nervous laughter began to spread through the room, as the audience tried to figure out what exactly I was doing. I thought, *well, so far so good, I'm getting a laugh ... but really, what I am I going to do?*

I broke the spell and announced, "Ladies and gentlemen, you do know, of course, that I don't really perform magic? Magic isn't real. These are tricks requiring extreme skill that are performed for your entertainment." I paused.

"But sometimes, little things go wrong, and ladies and gentlemen, this is one of those times. Something has indeed gone wrong, and it's entirely the fault of my assistant's husband. You see, I'm very sorry to say that this man has sabotaged part of your entertainment tonight, and I feel every bit as much a victim of his cruelty as you do. Would you like to know what this man has done—how exactly he's spoiled our fun?"

Silence filled the room. I stepped down from the stage, the small box still in my hand, and crossed the room to my nervously waiting assistant and her alarmed husband. I handed her the box and quietly asked her to open it with the key. She did, and the ring sparkled inside. I grasped it, held it above my head, and said, in a powerful, dramatic voice.

"I'll tell you what he's done. This man bought his beautiful wife a ring that's too big for this trick."

The audience roared with laughter, and the husband stood up and took a bow. I returned the ring to its rightful owner, smiled, and returned to the stage.

Once there, I announced, "Okay, now that that's over, can I get a volunteer with a cheap husband?"

The crowd went nuts. All around the room, hands shot into the air. Women shouted, "Me! Me!" I picked a woman with a considerably smaller ring, and the trick was a huge hit.

At the end of the show, I closed with a bang: "I just want to say one thing to all the ladies who let us know tonight that they have cheap husbands: I'm single and available after the show, but you'll have to drive. My parents won't let me have a car."

Once again, the crowd went wild. I got a standing ovation and lots of handshakes from the men and hugs from the ladies. It was a great night, and it's still one of my favorite memories. As my mother drove me home from the country club that night, I had a revelation. I turned to her and said,

"You know, if I hadn't been hit by a drunk driver, and if I hadn't gone through all of this pain and struggle, I never would have had this great night.

"Even though I was only a teenager, I was a successful professional magician. I loved it. I learned so much from this experience: how to tell a story, for example, and how to be comfortable on stage. All of my fears about public speaking disappeared—of course, truth be told, I don't know whether I ever really had them or not, but I certainly don't have any now. But then one day, I was done with magic. I had had enough. I loved it and treasured it as part of my past, but I stopped performing and sold everything I had—just like that.

Catching Up with Cathy

With being out an entire semester of school after the
accident, without Cathy I wouldn't have made my high
school graduation on schedule.

My hospitalization and recovery meant that I missed a lot of school—an entire semester, to be exact. Since I'd never been a great scholar, I knew that I'd be way behind the rest of my class when I eventually returned.

My mother and father sat down with me to discuss what to do: Should I plan to repeat the grade, or should they hire a tutor to come to our home every day and catch me up on what I'd been missing? They left the decision up to me, which was kind. I certainly didn't want to be held back a grade, so my mother consulted with the school's administration to find a tutor who could work with me, one on one. She found someone—Cathy was her name—and Mom told me that Cathy was a pretty blond woman. That sounded encouraging.

A week or so later, my sessions with Cathy began. Let's just say that a thirteen-year-old boy and a thirty-eight-year-old woman have different ideas of what "pretty" is, but Cathy was kind and, more importantly, very patient. Patience was not just a virtue in this case. It was necessary, given my work ethic at the time.

My idea of recovery was to sit around and watch TV, and prior to Cathy's arrival, that's just what I'd done. My mobility was very limited at first, of course, so I spent most of my time in bed, with the TV at my feet. What else was there to do?

Cathy had different ideas. Studying required me to focus, she said, and getting me to focus was pretty challenging with a TV blaring in the background. Pretty unreasonable, right?

In the end, of course, Cathy won that argument. My lessons with Cathy weren't particularly fun, but in hindsight, I have to admit that they weren't too bad, either. Most importantly, Cathy's guidance enabled me to keep up with my classmates, and I didn't have to repeat the grade.

I'd like to be able to say that the accident, and the months of recovery that followed, were the reasons I ended up as a C-minus student. But of course that's not true—after all, I already confessed to you that I'd had that streak going since kindergarten. I can't blame that on the accident, or Cathy, or anyone else: that's on me. Throughout my school days, whether I was in elementary, junior high, or high school, I never once cracked a book to study. I never even took them home from school! I always just squeaked by, getting through by winging it.

Up and Around

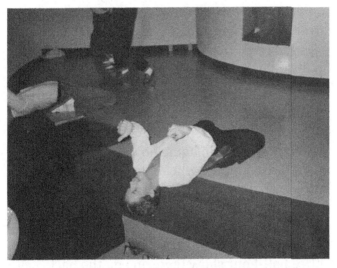

My first real business venture and disaster - a 1950's night club and buffet. I never could get away from the stage.

For a lot of my recovery process, I was bedridden or close to it. Every moment I spent in that bed entrenched a sense of restlessness, and those days made me long for the moment I'd be back up and around.

Eventually, I was able to get around in a wheelchair and later on crutches, and once I got the hang of them, I was off and running, so to speak. I'd been cooped up in the same spot for so long that I invested all of my energy—and then some—into figuring out how to get around and cover as much ground as I could. It was almost as if I'd stored all that energy, for months, and was finally able to expend it.

First up, let's talk about my expert use of the wheelchair. You know how kids enjoy tipping back in chairs, much to their parents' annoyance? Well, imagine how much fun a kid might have popping wheelies in a wheelchair. I'd blaze through the house, in and out of every room, all on the back wheels of the chair, and I'd do it just as fast as I could on all four wheels. I'd make TV time more interesting by watching an entire half-hour show teetering on the back wheels of the chair. I'd balance on those back wheels and spin in circles, making everyone who watched dizzy (but never me).

Once I'd graduated to crutches, I quickly learned how to zoom around nearly as fast as my classmates. The secret? Using the crutches exclusively and not letting my feet touch the floor. I could easily maneuver up and down steps, and I could even cruise all the way across my school gymnasium's floor—all crutches, no feet.

Restoring my mobility was a huge goal, and once it was complete, new challenges like returning to school loomed large. Life at school had gone on without me, of course, and transitioning back into the school environment after such a long period was kind of rough.

During my first meeting with the school principal before my return, he'd told me to leave each class five minutes early so I'd make it to the next class on time. I needed more space than the average student to get around, of course, and the halls were already packed between classes.

One day a few months into this routine, I stood and began to gather my things about five minutes before the end time of one of my classes. The teacher spotted me, stopped the lecture, and ordered me to sit back down. She then proceeded, in front of the entire class, to tell me that I was "no one special" and didn't need to leave class early anymore.

Later that same day, a classmate I'd long considered to be one of my closest friends added to the embarrassment and humiliation I'd suffered at the teacher's hands. In front of a group of other kids, he started to make fun of me, saying that the cast on my leg smelled bad. As the other kids started to laugh and egged him on, he ramped up his attack, going on and on about the stench.

It was beyond hurtful, in part because there was truth to what he'd said. The cause was an open ulcer on my lower leg that simply refused to heal. It was deep—I could sink my index finger into the sore as far as my first knuckle—and it bled and seeped fluids constantly. And yes, it smelled terrible. The seepage was so bad that it would soak through the cast every two weeks or so, and I'd have to go back to the hospital and have the wound cleaned and treated and get the cast replaced. I so looked forward to those days, even though they were painful, because at least it meant that the sore and cast wouldn't smell for a few days.

And of course what made the teasing worse was that the boy who'd singled me out, the one who mocked me, was someone who I'd called a friend literally since we were babies. He did it in public, in front of everyone. And I also thought of all the effort my mother put in to masking the smell because she knew how much it bothered it. Every morning, she'd wrap the cast in a new bandage and spray it with Lysol. She did so much to make it better, all to no avail. It was one of the many times I felt that no matter how she or I tried, we couldn't win.

No one hated the smell more than me. It hung around me like a black cloud, a constant reminder of what had happened to me, and of what was continuing to happen to me. But for someone I'd grown up with, someone I'd considered a friend, to make fun of me for it? I was devastated.

That afternoon, when I got home, all that humiliation took its toll. Before I even got to the front door, I started crying hysterically. I slumped over in the grass and began beating my crutches—which were both my ticket to freedom and an anchor weighing me down—over our fence. I slammed them, hard as I could, over and over against the pickets until the crutches splintered apart beyond repair.

Of course, I hadn't really thought things through before my outburst. Without those crutches, I wasn't going anywhere. I had no choice but to sit there, weeping, until someone came along to help me up and into the house.

To her credit, my mother let me sit there and wallow in my anger and self-pity for half an hour. She knew, instinctively, that I needed to get it out.

Finally, she came out, sat by my side in the grass, and asked me what had happened. I told her about the teacher's words, and then about the betrayal by my friend. She thought for a moment, hugged me, and said, "Devin, you just can't let stuff like this get to you. You're tougher than that."

I thought about what she'd said. I *was* tougher than that. Hadn't I been proving that every day since the accident? I'd proved it to everyone else, and now it was time for me to understand and accept it as true.

My mother helped me inside, and the next morning, she took me out to get a new set of crutches. I didn't look back, and neither did she.

The Stress on Us All

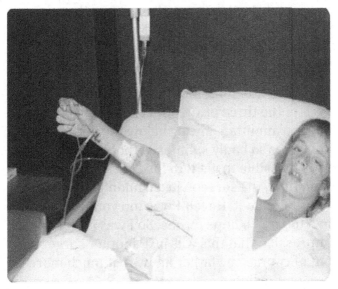

The trauma after the accident was so severe that my calf
swelled to double the size of my thigh. The medical staff
had to cut open my cast to avoid further injury.

Of course, stress was ever-present in my family throughout my recovery, and it affected us all differently. My father was a very serene man: always centered, always calm, and always consistent. But on one occasion, even he was pushed to his breaking point.

I remember it vividly: It was a lazy afternoon several months after the accident. My cast had been off the preceding two weeks in an effort to allow the open ulcer to heal. The ulcer had to completely heal for me to have a fourth and final surgery on my leg, the one that would hopefully allow the bone to fully fuse. The first three surgeries I'd undergone had been unsuccessful.

But there was something I didn't know. In fact, in each of the three prior surgeries, the plan had been to amputate my leg below the knee. The bone was so badly splintered that it just didn't seem possible to get it to fuse back together, but each time, the surgeon just couldn't bring himself to do it. He felt I was too young, and he had too much hope for me. So I was under the impression that this was just another surgery, but of course, my father knew that much more was on the line.

Since the cast had been removed, in many respects, I'd been back to square one. I wasn't allowed to move around without assistance. I couldn't go to school, or play outside, or do pretty much anything other than sit in a chair or lie in bed.

So there we were, Dad and I, sitting in our dining room and talking. I don't remember what it was that we were talking about, but it's what happened next that matters.

My leg had been hurting for some time, but as we talked that afternoon, the pain got considerably worse. It had been quite a while since the cast had been removed, and in many respects the pain was more acute—and certainly different—without it.

I asked Dad to slide the chair next to him over in front of me, so I could rest my leg on it. He did, and I raised up my leg to rest my foot on the chair. As I did, my leg bent backward, along the middle on my shin, and it wasn't just a little—it was a lot.

The pain was crystalline and so strange, that feeling of bone against bone. My stomach lurched as I cried out in agony. But Dad's reaction was even more dramatic. My steady, reliable father, the one who always held it together, simply broke. The man I knew as the voice of calmness and reason clapped his hand to his mouth, ran to the bathroom, and threw up.

As I sat there, contorted in pain, I heard him shout something, as loud as he could, that I never thought I'd hear him say—that he wanted to kill the man who had done this to me.

The physical and emotional pain overwhelmed me, and I broke down and cried. I was so confused, so tired of this THING I was going through. It was so unfair that I had to suffer, and that my family had to suffer. I just wanted it all to end.

Getting MADD

Officer Kent Gabrielson (the first officer on the scene of the accident) noting one of the points of impact where my jean fibers left an imprint in the steel bumper of the car that struck me.

When I was seventeen, my parents invited me to join them at a lecture presented by a local chapter of Mothers Against Drunk Driving (MADD). The speaker that night was a local businessman—a guy who wore a suit and tie to work every day, drove a nice car, and worked in a nice office. He was a respected man, but he'd been arrested for drunk driving and taken to jail. He'd been strip-searched and placed in a detox area of the jail along with, I recall him saying, "all the other criminals." He recounted that the experience had been the most incredibly frightening, humiliating thing he could ever imagine going through. He said that he vividly remembered telling the officer, "But I only had three drinks."

As part of the businessman's community-service sentence, he was required to make a public service announcement video. The video was only a few minutes long, but it had been professionally produced. In the video, a man very much like the evening's speaker—clearly a big shot—is depicted on his way to work, at the office, and then driving home. As he drives home, down a residential street, kids are playing all around in the yards of the neighborhood. As he's nearing his own home, a ball rolls out into the street, and a small girl runs after it, directly in the path of his car. A second later, blood spatters on the windshield.

I lost it. I broke down and started crying—sobbing, really. Everything I had gone through came rushing back to me. It was a devastating feeling: I had no idea that that much emotion could hit me so suddenly, at what felt like the speed of light. All eyes turned to look at me, but I couldn't hold it together.

After I finished blubbering, someone in the group who knew what I'd been through asked if I'd get up and speak about what had happened to me. So I did.

"I was a victim of a drunk driver a few years ago."

I looked at the speaker. "I want you to know that I don't hate you. I don't think you're a bad person. Alcohol is alcohol. It's not good or bad. It's what we do after we drink it that can create a good or bad situation."

The businessman wept as I spoke for the next ten minutes. It was quite emotional for everyone in the room.

As my parents and I were on our way out of the meeting that evening, a man stopped me.

"Devin, I want to talk to you." I paused.

"My name is Dick. I'm a serious offenders' probation officer."

That made me curious. "Serious offenders, meaning what?"

"Well, offenders convicted of repeated drunk driving offenses. I'm a probation officer for people who have been arrested and convicted three or more times."

"Okay, what do you want from me?"

Dick replied, "Well, I want you to go give talks with me about your experience. Clearly, you're very comfortable speaking to people. You have a very good story, and you have a very healthy attitude about it. I'd like you to do this with me."

I thought for a moment before responding. "Sure. Here's our number. Call me."

A few weeks later, Dick called. "I've got an engagement to speak at a high school. I want you to go with me."

The talk was indeed at a local high school. Dick and I were to speak before fifty to sixty kids. As the date for the talk neared, I thought a lot about how to tell my story, but quite intentionally, I didn't practice. Ultimately, I decided to give them facts and statistics and not tell them that I had been a victim of a drunk-driving accident up front.

I told Dick, "Don't let them know I was in an accident. And make sure the teacher doesn't introduce me as somebody who's been in an accident. I want them to think of me as someone who's going to talk about drunk driving, period."

My thought process was this: if I walked in that classroom and told them, "Alcohol's bad. Don't ever drink," I knew they'd immediately shut down and stop listening.

Instead, I started by saying, "I want to tell you a story. On October first, in 1976, a young man went for a bike ride." For the next ten minutes, I relayed the story of the accident, and then moved on to the statistics.

"The accident I just described was what is referred to as a personal injury caused by drunk driving. It may surprise you, but more than 750,000 of these incidents occur every year in this country. The injuries involved vary, but 35,000 of them result in a death each year."

I continued, "Now, the particular story I told you is only one of these incidents, okay? But the reason I know this story so well is because I *am* that young man."

Seconds after I said those words, a young man seated in the front row fell straight forward out of his chair, hit his head on the floor, and lay there, unconscious. I didn't know what to do—I hadn't been trained in CPR or first aid. I stood there, dumbfounded.

The teacher ran to him right away, and someone called for the school nurse. The nurse came down, and as the classroom buzzed with activity, a young woman said that she felt like she was going to faint, too. As she began to slump out of her chair, she fell to her knees. Both of them were removed from the classroom.

Rattled but committed to tell the audience the whole story, I finished the talk. As we were leaving, the teacher stopped me.

She said, "I want you to know that those two are going to be fine. It's just that your story hit them so hard that they passed out."

I didn't quite know what to do with that, so I apologized.

She replied, "No, Devin. You don't have to apologize. The reason I'm telling you this is that you have an incredible story. You have passion, and you have a way of telling your story that you must continue."

"You need to keep talking, and you need to tell your story to as many people as you can," she continued.

Emboldened, I continued accepting offers to give talks. I spoke before church, school, and neighborhood groups; companies; and even fraternities and sororities at the university down the road from where I lived. It was pretty wild how many I did.

With each presentation, I'd give the story a little different spin, but I'd always deliver it in a way to ensure the full impact resonated with my listeners. Every time I would give a talk, some of the attendees would come up and hug me, and there'd always be tears. Honestly, I didn't quite know how to deal with all the emotions.

Eventually, interest expanded to the point where I was delivering presentations to the entire student bodies of schools—as many as four to five hundred people at a time. In one instance, I was invited to present to the Iowa Crime Prevention Association—my biggest crowd ever, with six hundred police officers in the room. I spoke to the group for three hours, nonstop, and I got a standing ovation. It was incredible. Sometime later, I spoke before the Iowa Police Chiefs Convention, and then again at a conference on drunk driving set up by the governor of Iowa. The interest in having me speak to groups never seemed to let up.

For each presentation I delivered, I tried to customize a different approach or spin that was tailored just to the group I'd be facing. I always wanted to truly speak to my audience, to be sure that my message would stay with them after it was over. So when Dick invited me to speak to a group session of eight to twelve men who were "serious offenders" (that is, people with three or more drunk-driving convictions), I thought hard about what would leave the deepest impression.

I asked Dick for help in how to approach the presentation—what specifically I should talk about, and for how long. Dick smiled, told me I had up to half an hour, and assured me that I'd think of something. I mulled it over for a few days before deciding what to do.

In the days leading up to the talk, I asked a friend whose parents were beer drinkers (mine weren't) to save a box for a twelve-pack of beer and the empty cans as well. Just like any magician, I needed some props to make a strong impression.

When I walked into the session, a brown bag containing the box and empty beer cans in my hand, I found the group seated in a semicircle. No one noticed my presence or paid any attention for a while, so I listened quietly for a break in the conversation.

When one finally came, I bypassed the podium, pulled up a chair, and joined the circle. The group silently watched as I reached into the bag and pulled out what appeared to be a twelve-pack of Budweiser. I held it in front of me and looked around the circle.

Well, I had their attention. The room was very quiet. I waited a few moments and then stood, raised the box up high, and ripped it in half; as I did, the cans clattered to the floor and rolled about.

A moment or so passed until one man exclaimed, "What the hell is this all about?"

I asked the group, "What do you see here?"

Silence returned, until someone said. "Just a bunch of empty cans." Another said, "Looks like I missed the party" and laughed; a few other comments followed.

I said, "Can I tell you what I see?"

I bent to pick up a can. I held it up and said, "When I look at this one, I see a broken family."

I set the can aside and picked up another.

"In this one, I see shattered dreams."

I continued with each can, telling the story of each: really expensive car insurance, a lost license, a bad car accident, a lost job, a few nights in jail. In all, it took about ten minutes to tell the stories of eleven of the cans.

Next, I picked up a can and made a great show of studying it. I put it back and then sifted through the others until I found the one I hadn't told the story of, the one that was dented and worn and in bad shape. I held it out in the light, before my audience, dramatically, methodically.

I said, "Let me tell you what I see in this one. This is a special one." I handed the can to the man seated next to me and told him to hold it for a few minutes as I talked before passing it to the next man. I told the men that I wanted each of them to hold on to the can for a while as they listened, and that at the end of the story, I planned to ask them a question.

With that, I began to tell my personal story, but I didn't tell them that I was the victim. I took them through the whole story, all thirty to forty minutes, but I didn't mention that a drunk driver was at fault. Honestly, they were all so engrossed in the story that I doubted any of them even gave it a thought. In this telling, this was just another car versus bicycle accident with a sad end.

By the time the story was over, the can had made its way around the circle and was back in my hands. I held it above my head and said, "In this can, I see the driver in the story. He was drunk when the accident happened—three times the legal limit."

I tossed the can into the hands of the man sitting across from me and asked the man next to me to pick the cleanest, most whole can he could find in the group and to hand it to me.

I studied the can the man gave me and said, "In this can, I see the boy in the story. He's young, clean, unscathed. He's perfect."

With that, I put the can on the floor and suddenly stomped it flat.

"And this is what happened to him. This is the boy after the accident. Remember what I told you about the splintered bones in his leg, and the 250 stitches needed to sew his wounds back together?"

I rolled up my jeans.

"This is him now. This is what his leg looks like now."

For several minutes, no one in the group made a sound. Then the silence was broken by the sound of weeping.

I stood and said, in a very soft voice, "Gentlemen, the man who hit me that day didn't leave work with a plan to cause me harm. He didn't plan to do what he did, but it happened, and it can happen to you."

"You can drink and you can drive, but you can't do both at the same time." With that, I walked out.

The next day, the director of the group called to thank me, and also to tell me what a strong effect my story had had on the men in the group. Sometime later, he called me again to share that he'd been shocked by the amount of energy and investment the group members had for the rest of the sessions. He knew it was my story that had made all the difference.

Experiences like these honed my presentation skills and made me very passionate about what I was doing. I'd always assumed that my passion stemmed from the fact that it was a very personal story, and thus it was important to me. But later, I realized how integral the talks were to my healing process. I was spreading this message in an effort to help other people avoid the misfortune I'd had.

My message was simple: you don't have to be a bad person to be a drunk driver. All it takes is having a little bit too much to drink and misplacing trust in your compromised reasoning skills for one critical moment. It really could happen to anyone.

What Failure Taught Me

My second business venture, a fine dining establishment, and second failure. After this restaurant closed, I went through personal bankruptcy but learned a lot about business and how to focus on the right parts to ensure success.

My speaking career went on for a while, but eventually I felt the need to slow things down. After the last few, I stopped, and I didn't return to speaking about my experience for quite some time.

High school ended for me—as I mentioned, with a C-minus record—and I decided that college wasn't for me. I didn't like school: I paid little attention while I was there and wasn't a good student, probably by a lot of measures. I knew what I wanted to do instead. I wanted to go into business.

For pretty much my whole life, I'd dreamed of becoming a carpenter or of working in construction. I loved the idea of building things that would last. But while I was still in my cast and just getting around on crutches, my doctors tried to crush that dream.

"Devin," they told me, "you're never going to be able to do that. You're not going to be able to work in construction. Your body can't take it. You've had too many injuries. You just can't do it."

As I internalized this message at that young age—still in my early teens—I took the same attitude I'd had the day my parents told me not to go on that fateful bike ride. I thought, "Well, I appreciate that, but I'm going to do it anyway. I'm going to work in construction. I've known this my whole life, and I'm not going to change my plans now. I'm going to be a contractor."

Fortunately, my high school offered classes and training in the field. While I was still in school, I helped build a house as a project. After high school, I began doing odd jobs in construction: hanging drywall and doors, installing windows and roofing houses.

All the while, I was dealing with immense pain on a constant basis, just as I had ever since the accident. Eventually, though, I began to notice that the type of work I was doing was exacerbating the pain beyond the point I could stand.

I made a conscious decision at the beginning of my recovery process that I wasn't going to take pain medications. I learned different ways to deal with the pain, but I was afraid of the idea of adding a drug addiction to the fallout of my injuries. Part of my aversion to medications came about as a result of the violent reactions I'd had to certain medications I received in the hospital. Even in such a controlled environment, with people around me constantly to take care of me, the medications had terrible consequences. I'd also heard a lot about celebrities and athletes who had gotten hooked on pain medications, and how it often led to their undoing. So I decided to forgo the whole idea.

I saw a lot of chiropractors. I saw a lot of doctors. I saw a lot of pain specialists. I learned self-hypnosis techniques and many concentration exercises, and I practiced them multiple times a week. Nonetheless, the pain was always there. It took on a life of its own, and I found that it wasn't under my control.

One day, I faced the fact that I couldn't continue working in construction. The doctor had been right. I couldn't do it. I had to figure something else out and let my dream go. Even though I'd had the dream for as long as I could remember— even as a small child—I had to let it go.

So I did. I went into business for myself. I'd worked odd jobs in restaurants as a kid— cooking, washing dishes, that sort of thing—and I liked the restaurant business.

The first restaurant I opened failed miserably. Of course, my stubborn, I-can-do-it attitude hadn't diminished in the slightest. I thought, "Well, now I know what *doesn't* work, so that must mean that now I know what *will* work. I'm going to try again." I tried again and bought a restaurant that was for sale. I operated it for a while, and it too ended in failure.

While my business was failing, I was still working very hard at it—around fifty to sixty hours a week. Yet I realized that I had to look for another job that would pay my bills. I hunted through the help-wanted section of the newspaper and eventually found a job in door-to-door sales of health insurance to rural families.

Around the same time I started the insurance job, my second restaurant venture sputtered to an end, and I was forced to close it. I didn't care for the job selling insurance, but I did fall in love with the mechanism of insurance. I began to study the history of the field—the "friendly society" that Benjamin Franklin had formed when he came to the New World—and learned the different ways that it worked and evolved. I found that I was fascinated by it.

It soon became evident to me that modern society, as we know it today, could not exist without insurance. Think of the costs involved with cars, homes, commercial buildings, and so on. No one would risk borrowing or lending such vast sums of money for their purchase if the purchases weren't insured in some way. In a way, insurance is woven into the fabric of modern life. I wanted to be sure I became a part of it.

How Insurance
Revived My Passion

Myself, my son Jacob and Jim Craig at the Master
Builders of Iowa (AGC) Annual Conference. I was the
Master of Ceremonies and introduced Mr. Craig at the
event. Mr. Craig is a retired American ice hockey
goaltender who was part of the 1980 U.S. Olympic
hockey team that won the Olympic gold medal at the
Lake Placid Winter Games, otherwise known as the
"Miracle on Ice." Craig stopped 36 of 39 shots during
that game as the U.S. beat the Soviets, 4-3.

I quickly tired of door-to-door sales, and I longed to be part of an office environment. I left that first job and began selling home and auto insurance to individuals. It passed the time, but I soon became much more interested in insurance sales to small commercial enterprises.

As I gained more experience in selling to small commercial businesses, I found that I was quite good at it and expanded my reach to larger commercial businesses and contractors. The company I was working for didn't cater to such large enterprises, so I ended up going to a larger independent agency. There, I became a partner very quickly. My sales figures exceeded those of everyone else in the company, so I had the ability to work exclusively with businesses, rather than individuals.

I loved it. As I'd suffered through the failure of two businesses, I understood many of the difficulties and challenges faced by my business-owner clients too. Because of this, I could relate them differently than my colleagues who hadn't had similar experiences. This created a deep level of trust—a bond—with my clients, who ultimately depended on me as a trusted partner.

At the same time, I didn't feel comfortable with the direction the agency I worked for was going. The firm's leadership seemed resistant to change and improvement and uninterested in building the company into something more significant.

So I left, at the young age of forty-two. I cashed in my retirement, sold my shares in the company, and risked everything on an idea: becoming a specialist.

I'd long wanted to work exclusively with contractors. I knew that they were the clients I felt most comfortable with. I liked that they were direct. I liked that they were hard to service. I liked that they were demanding. I liked that doing business with them was very, very complicated, and I was up to the challenge. I felt that if I was going to pick an industry to specialize in, why not pick the one that's most difficult?

Perhaps it was hubris. I didn't fully understand how all-consuming the decision would be when I made it. I thought it meant that I'd do nothing but call on contractors, and that that would be it.

Well, I realized pretty quickly that it wasn't quite that simple. My decision to specialize meant driving past a hundred prospects on my way to get to one. I learned that I'd better have a pretty good story when I got to that one potential client.

In fact, I ended up spending a couple of years with my current company building a platform before I made any calls at all. The process involved a lot of trial and error, including conducting extensive interviews with contractors in which I discovered what they truly needed from our industry. And it worked: eventually, when the full service platform was in place, I was able to draw on this extensive body of knowledge as I sold to contractors. We did very well and attracted lots of business on a local scale. And as we continued on, we got better and better and better at what we did.

As I reflected on where we were, and what the nature of the business was, I began to have some reservations. Suddenly, I felt uncomfortable with the idea of continuing in the same way, as a mostly solo effort. Instead, I wanted to build a group of people who do the work, at a scale where it could go nationwide. I started trying to figure out how to replicate processes and scale the model, while at the same time providing even better service to our clients and enticing good people to join and stay on our team.

I had no notion at the time of what a mammoth task this would be, but I did know from past experience that if I trusted in myself, and if I worked hard at it, I could make it work.

And so we did, now as a team of twelve servicing contractors of various sizes and disciplines in thirty-six of these United States. While our team works hard for our clients, I have the flexibility to travel the country and give lectures about business, insurance, and types of construction— which in turn attracts even more business.

This has all gone very well, of course. We've built a strong and thriving business. It's also integral to the story of how my transformative experience—the accident—has led me to become what I am today. Along the way, I was rarely aware of how I was getting to this place. I was just on my way.

Back in the Hospital

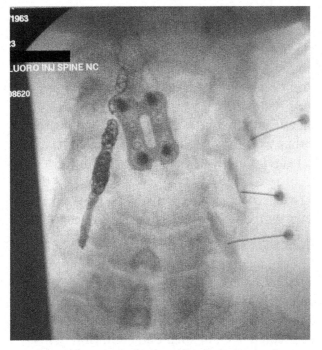

X-ray of my neck showing the plate that broke my
vertebrae after my surgical disc replacement. The screws
along with the sealed vertebral artery are also visible.

The first ten to fifteen years after the accident was mostly a fight to stay alive, to keep my head above water. The pain was, and still is, severe, every minute of every day. To this day, I wake up six to eight times during a night to find both arms completely numb; in fact, I never sleep more than a couple of hours at a time.

I still don't take pain medication, and I don't believe I ever will.

A struggle with pain is a constant battle, as it takes on a life of its own and becomes part of you. I doubt that I'll ever get used to it, but I have learned to deal with it. A turning point came in September 2011, when another medical crisis occurred. I had ruptured a disc in my neck, which is a relatively common occurrence. As it happens, thanks to advances in medicine and good surgeons, the fix for it is relatively reliable, too. The disc would be replaced with cadaver tissue, and a steel plate would be placed on my vertebrae, along with two screws at the C3 disc and two screws at the C4 disc. The plate and screws would hold the vertebrae in place until healing would fuse it all together.

But because my neck had been broken before and hadn't healed well, for me, the fix wasn't so simple. When the surgeon initially went in, he had to halt the surgery; he later told me that he'd never seen a neck in such bad condition in his career. My vertebrae were angled in a way that they shouldn't be, which of course had led to the ruptured disc. The surgeon had to literally muscle it back into place to get the plate on. While the surgery was successful, the aftermath was anything but.

Two carotid and two vertebral arteries transfer blood to the brain. A phenomenon known as the circle of Willis allows for collateral flow between them, providing blood to the brain. The morning after surgery, my vertebrae shifted back and broke where the titanium plate and screws were located. As a result of the break, one of the screws began pressing so hard against my left vertebral artery that it became sealed, causing two strokes.

I was rushed into surgery at the University of Iowa Hospital's Neuro Unit with no idea why or what they were doing—or even how dangerous the situation was. As it would turn out, I was lucky again— but for perhaps the third or fourth time, I faced a potentially life-threatening situation.

The surgical team briefed me. It was a disaster: a rebroken neck, a sealed vertebral artery, two strokes, and perhaps worst of all, a sharp screw pressing on a critical artery.

"Devin," the surgeon said, "Here's the problem. You have this screw in your neck. It's pointed, and it's pressing against a main artery of your brain. It will pierce it eventually—why it hasn't pierced it yet, we don't know, but it definitely will. When it does, you'll have a massive bleed-out, and you'll die immediately."

"Okay. So, what's the procedure?"

The surgeon paused. "Well … we don't have a procedure for this. We've never seen anything like it before, so we're not sure."

That was sobering news. I replied, "Well, okay then. What are we going to do?"

"There's only one person we're comfortable with handling this surgery, and he's out of the country right now."

I blinked, taking all the bad news in. "Wow. The punches keep coming."

"Well, we've gotten a hold of him, and he's on his way back. We're going to keep you in intensive care until he returns—but if something happens in the meantime, there's probably nothing we can do. We're keeping you in the ICU because we want to keep as close an eye on you as we can."

I lay there, in intensive care, for a few days. The night before the surgeon's impending return, the anesthesiologist came in to talk to me.

"Devin, this is going to be a difficult surgery, and it's one that we're not certain about."

I looked at him. "What do you mean?"

He replied, "Well, the outcome of it. We're unsure about it. You need to prepare yourself."

His vagueness made me angry. "What in the hell does that mean? Prepare myself for what?"

"You need to prepare yourself and your family for what will happen if you don't wake up."

I definitely wasn't sure how to deal with that, but I dealt with it all the same. I asked my father, my wife, and my son to talk with me about it after the doctor left. They didn't want to, but I insisted.

"We're *going* to talk about this."

I told them my wishes, including what I wanted for each of them, and briefly discussed the whereabouts and contents of my will. It was very emotional, but ultimately, we decided to leave everything, including our trust, in the hands of the competent medical staff—and God.

When the surgeon finally arrived, I was hauled out of the ICU, bed and all, and rushed to the OR. It was nothing new for me, of course—at this point in my life, I'd already been through ten surgeries.

But once we got to the OR, this one was very different. I'd never seen more than four people in an OR before; if during one of my previous operations, more people than that had been present, they'd come in after I was unconscious. This OR was teeming with people, all in a mad rush. It was very chaotic, and it scared me. I lay there, watching, my eyes scuttling back and forth with all the motion.

Suddenly, I screamed, "Stop!" and they did. I don't think they knew who was yelling, but sure enough, everyone stopped, turned, and looked at me.

I said, "You all are scaring me. I'd like you guys to gather around the bed for a minute."

One by one, each of them all set their stuff down and slowly walked over to the bed. I'm sure they were thinking, "What is this?"

I had played this game before. I started by telling a couple of jokes. I'm sure they weren't very good ones—they didn't get much of a laugh, maybe a couple of chuckles here and there. But then I told them that I hoped they all believed in God, as I do, because as confident as I was in their individual talents, I had the confidence of knowing that we had God on our side, too.

A young lady stood at the end of the bed. She squeezed my feet through the blanket and said, "Devin, we have to get going now. We're in a bit of a hurry."

As the anesthesiologist began administering the juice that would make me sleep through it all, others began to strap me down. I don't recall whether I'd been strapped down during any of my previous ten surgeries; if so, it happened after I was out.

But I was awake for this, and it intensified my fear. It all roiled inside my head: the conversations with the anesthesiologist and then with my family the night before; the jarring sight of so many people in the room; and then the frightening process of being strapped down. Just as they placed the last strap around my head, I succumbed to the anesthesia.

After it was over, the surgeon found my family in the hallway. He said, "We have a miracle boy on our hands."

My father looked at him with surprise and relief. "What do you mean, 'a miracle boy'?"

He said, "Well, we've only tried this procedure twice, and neither patient made it. They both passed away during the surgery."

"Your son is alive."

Becoming the Author of My Story

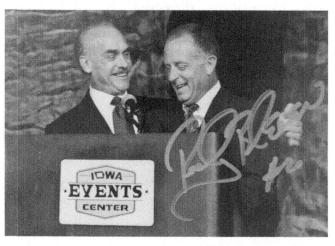

Myself and Rocky Bleier sharing a laugh before he took the stage as the guest speaker at the Master Builders of Iowa (AGC) Annual Conference. Robert Patrick "Rocky" Bleier is an former professional football player. He was a National Football League halfback for the Pittsburgh Steelers in 1968 and from 1971 to 1980 and has four Super Bowl Championships.

The first few months following that surgery were the most mentally and physically draining moments of my life. During one particularly low point, I began to believe that this would be my new normal: feeling, acting, and looking like an old, feeble man who couldn't take care of himself.

This new "reality" was horrible. There's no way I could have ever prepared for such a situation, and to be sure, I *wasn't* prepared for what I went through. This thought—that this would be my new normal—was the most terrifying part.

I didn't believe I'd come out of it, but I did. That's a whole other story, of course, but I did return to my "old normal," and I was grateful for it.

One day a year or so afterward, I took some time to reflect on what I'd been through. I wondered *how* I'd come out of it and *how* I had ever arrived at a point where I was happy again and had put it behind me. And that's where the story within the story comes to fruition.

Through all of my experiences over the preceding forty-one years, I had felt like my story was being written for me. As I moved through my life, I truly believed I was simply following along the sentences and the paragraphs and the pages and the chapters that had been scripted for me.

With a fresh perspective, I realized that wasn't what had happened at all. In fact, I had put to good use all the many lessons my parents had taught me about self-reliance. I had drawn from the reserves of courage I had built through letting my dream go and allowing a new dream to blossom in its place. I was strengthened by the years of practice I'd had of presenting to groups. I benefited from the knowledge I'd gathered on relating to others through the talks I'd given and the magic shows I'd performed. I capitalized on the lessons I'd learned from my two failed business ventures. I was open-minded enough to let myself fall in love with the world of insurance. I was brave enough to risk it all and become a specialist.

I finally realized that through all of these trials and tribulation, at each moment that something bad happened to me, I had subconsciously told myself, "Devin, you can choose to be a *victim* or a *victor*." Being a victim didn't sit well with me, so I'd always chosen to be a victor instead.

For years, I'd said to myself, "This accident and this pain will not define me." But one day, I made an active choice to change my message: "Yes, this accident and this pain absolutely *does* define me, but I get to decide *how* it does." And how it defines me is as a victor. I will never be a victim.

Whenever these bad things happened, I searched my mind and my heart for a way that I could use the experience to change my life for the positive. And every time I came out on the other side of the experience, I could honestly say, "I'm glad that happened, because if it hadn't, I wouldn't have made the decisions I made, which have gotten me to where I am today." I firmly believe that what we are, and who we are, are products of everything that has happened to us in the past.

It was only two years ago that it finally hit me. *I'm not following pages in my life's book, pages that somebody else has written. I've been the author all along. I've decided what the next chapter will be—even before it happens.*

In some cases, my foreshadowing was clear, and in others, it wasn't. But all along, I was always the sole author of this story. I had made a conscious choice to be a victor, rather than a victim, and it made all the difference. And if I hadn't realized all this and decided to write it all down—for real this time—you wouldn't be reading this book and learning how you, too, can be the author of your own life. Choosing to become a victor is a mindset. Bad stuff is going to happen to you: you can count on it. So be your author, be a victor, and write your own chapters.

If I'd never dared to dream of a life in construction, I wouldn't have had a dream to chase. If the accident hadn't happened, I wouldn't have learned how to overcome the hardest obstacles life could throw my way. If my mother hadn't given me the gift of magic, I never would have learned how to be comfortable in front of groups or how to relate to others. If I'd skipped that MADD meeting and never encountered the probation officer, I wouldn't have honed my public-speaking skills. If I hadn't found the courage to start two businesses, I wouldn't have learned the tremendously useful knowledge their failures gave me. If my businesses hadn't failed, I wouldn't have gotten into insurance. If I hadn't found my place in the world of insurance and decided to be a specialist, I wouldn't be back in construction—which had been my original dream. And that is the true meaning of full circle: my dream is fulfilled, despite the twisting path I took to reach it.

How is the book of my life going to end? I don't know, but I know I'm going to like it. I know bad things are going to happen to me, but I also know that I'll make decisions as a consequence of each of those situations that will make the next chapter of my life better. I'm going to keep writing this book for as long as God keeps me here.

My hope is that you will apply this message to your own life. I had a dream of being in the field of construction, and fate tried to rip it away from me. But I decided to be the victor. I wrote my own chapters, and today, I am a part of the world of construction. Sure, it isn't how I originally imagined it ... but I can't imagine anything better than my life is now.

All of us have the power to make our lives come full circle. Go ahead and let all the bad things define you: as a victor, not a victim. *No one* can take that away from you.

Becoming the Victor in Life

As part of my hard work and diligence that led to a
successful insurance career, I was fortunate to be
awarded a trip aboard the Silversea Silver Muse as it
cruised through the Mediterranean. I'm at the back of
the ship while my sister, whom I took as my plus one
and whose bike I "borrowed", is snapping the
photo. (aren't I a great brother?)

Bad things happen to all of us. Life has a way of bringing us to our knees when we least expect it. I've learned the hard way, from picking myself up from the side of the road after being hit by a drunk driver, that you in fact do have choices. You can choose to become a victim when life knocks you down, or you can look past it and turn it around. You can become a victor instead and use the experience as fuel to help become the author of your own story.

I used to tell myself to never let the bad things that happen define me. But after many surgeries, and after living with crippling pain, day in and day out, I've learned to embrace whatever life throws at me and to absolutely let it define me. I've learned how to turn the horrible things life throws at me into good things.

We've all heard the saying, "What doesn't kill you makes you stronger." But you may wonder: how can I take something truly horrible—living with a debilitating disease, say, or dealing with the death of a loved one—and find something positive in it? In this book, I've walked you through the story of my transformative experience, of being hit by a drunk driver and being on the brink of death, to where I am today: I'm a partner in a thriving company, and in a position to pave the way for others to shed the victim label and take control of their own destinies.

Time and again, I've been asked what my secret is; how do I turn the negative events that have happened to me over the course of my life into positive energy. If you ask me, I'll look you in the eye and tell you the same thing I've told others: "Because I decided that they would be."

It's that defining mindset that separates those who give up and who think life is unfair from those who grab life by the horns and turn tragedies into blessings. Your toughest lessons in life will always define you, one way or another. If you get through it, you've proven that you have the courage and the strength to overcome adversity.

You don't have to stay down. You don't have to be a victim of whatever life sends your way. Accept the bad things and turn them around. Wear with pride the fact that you've triumphed over your troubles.

Be the victor.

If you'd like Devin to be a key note speaker for your organization about how to be a victor, or to tell him about how his story impacted your life, please contact him at: **devin@rdcsolutions.org**

About the Author

Devin H. Pipkin has more than twenty years of experience in helping construction companies. He coordinates and manages multiple areas of risk that include contracts, certificates of insurance, human resources, safety/loss control, succession planning, trusted-advisor coordination and alternative risk financing. He frequently works on mergers and acquisitions as a consultant and facilitator.

As a member of multiple construction organizations, Devin is aware of the issues that contractors face today. He has held many board positions in the Cedar Rapids area, evidence of his dedication to his community.

Devin is an active mentor, providing professional coaching and development services to his team and clients.

He also teaches risk management and insurance for several industry associations with the goal of raising the bar in both insurance and construction.

If you'd like Devin to talk about how to be a victor at your organization, please contact him at **devin@rdcsolutions.org** and visit his website, **www.rdcsolutions.org**.

Made in the USA
Monee, IL
11 February 2021